C000221739

SUPERNATURAL STORIES OF THE WEST MIDLANDS

Birmingham and Solihull

Neil Kirby

Via Kindle

A special thank you to everyone who has helped with content for this book, especially my family 'The Kirby's' and even more especially my wife, Rachael.

....

All the following stories are reported as being true, some have photographs attached. The names of some of the people involved have been changed and some properties have intentionally not been mentioned. Most of them are located around the West Midlands where my family are from. Some are from our travels to other towns or countries.

The stories have been passed to me from trusted family members, good friends and colleagues from my days working in the police service and ambulance trust. Some are personal experiences.

I have written this book to share some of these stories with you and let you decide.

LOVELY OLD COUPLE. SMALL HEATH, BIRMINGHAM.

From 2010, when working in the ambulance service, talk of the supernatural would arise every now and then. I was told the following story by a colleague which interested me and sent a shiver down my spine.

An ambulance had been called to an address in Small Heath, on the outskirts of Birmingham city centre. As the crew entered the 1950's, terraced house, they noticed dusty antiques and old black and white photographs of the patient and her husband when they were newlywed, some fifty odd years prior.

The old lady had been feeling unwell and following a telephone call with her doctor, an ambulance had been booked to escort the lady into hospital for some routine tests. After completing a basic check-up prior to the journey and filling in the relevant paperwork the paramedic asked the old lady if he could pay a visit to the toilet.

Having ascended the stairs to the first floor where the bathroom was, the paramedic, Bob, bumped into the old lady's husband coming out of a bedroom. The old man who was clearly slow on his feet shuffled toward the clinician asking if Mable was going to be okay. Bob reassured the husband and informed him that the tests were routine following a period of feeling unwell. The old boy smiled and nodded and asked if Bob could pass on his love to his wife for him as he could not come down the stairs to see her.

The paramedic finished his business and returned to his crew mate who had assisted the old lady into a wheelchair and getting ready to travel. As the three of them were moving onto the vehicle, Bob smiled as he caught sight of the old man standing in the bedroom window waving his wife off. Bob smiled up to the husband and nodded as he pushed Mable onto the ambulance.

On the way into hospital, to break up the silence of the journey, Bob asked Mable how long she and her husband had been married. Bob was astonished when she replied that it would have been fifty-five years that coming June had Arthur still been alive. Bob sat in stunned, silence as Mable explained how her husband had been her only love until he died 6 months prior of a heart attack in their bedroom at home. She added, "I still feel that he's with me all the time".

VICTORIA ROAD, ASTON.

One cold morning in September 1971, two ladies were on Victoria road in Aston. They were either walking to work or waiting for a bus to take them to work when they both noticed a young woman wearing what was described as a 'green, frilly dress' standing in the middle of the road. Both women could see the woman and watched in terror as a bus approached her and was just about to hit the woman when she vanished in front of their eyes. When the bus had passed, they could see no sign of the young lady.

Some months later, another woman was passing the same stretch of road, only this time later on the evening. She also described seeing a young woman in a green dress crossing the road quickly towards her. As she watched the woman approach, she said she simply disappeared in front of her eyes.

Some reports state this apparition may be that of a young woman who worked as an usher at the nearby Victoria Playhouse Cinema, which closed in 1963. The woman was reported to have been knocked down by a car and killed when trying to cross the road, some years before.

FACE IN THE WINDOW. SOLIHULL.

During the late 1980's, an old school friend Dean, recalls an experience that shook his mother to the core and caused her to leave her cleaning job on the day it happened.

Dean was around seven years old at the time and his mom, Sue, was a cleaner. She worked at various large houses around Solihull. On this particular occasion, it was the summer holidays and she had taken her son to work with her. It was a relatively a new cleaning job at a large house in the Solihull countryside. She had only been given this new property recently by the cleaning agency as no other cleaners seemed to stay there for very long. She had been there a couple of times before and thought it was a little far away and this might have been the reason the other cleaners did not stay. The distance did not bother Sue and she enjoyed the run throught the country roads

The house was a large, rural property, with three floors. The third floor was within the roof of the house and contained two bedrooms and a children's nursery which had large, dormer windows , in which was perfect to safely leave Dean to play for a while whilst she went around her cleaning duties.

The owners of the property were a middle-aged couple who commuted into London daily and as so were rarely around during the cleaning. Sue recalls it had been a pleasant, mid-summers day as she used her keys to unlock the large oak door before entering the property which had been secure and the house empty at the time. She deactivated the alarm system and went around her cleaning tasks. This usually started with walking through to the back of the house and out the back door in order to bring in the washing from the rear garden.

Dean had continued up the two flights of stairs to the nursery which was packed with children's toys belonging to the owner's children who spent most of their time at a relatives house during the school holidays, whilst their parents worked.

As Sue folded the clean washing into a basket, she glanced up at Dean through the large dormer window and could see that he had already found toy planes which he was holding up, swishing them through the air.

She continued her way through her daily duties, working her way from room to room. Occasionally she checked in on him to ensure he was okay, she also took him some lunch about halfway through her shift, which would last a couple of hours or so.

After lunch and as her shift was drawing to an end, Sue was taking the rubbish which she had bagged up, out to the bins which were situated to the side of the house. As She walked across the large rear patio area, she again glanced up towards the nursery and saw Dean stood at the window. She waved to her son as he waved back.

At that moment, Sue's attention moved to an anomaly which felt out of place in the corner of her eye. Her attention had been drawn to the dormer window of the upper bedroom which was immediately next door to the nursery.

Sue felt a wave of coldness sweep over her as she found herself looking into the sunken eyes of a grey faced old man. The man was staring at her from the bedroom window. The stare lasted for several seconds before the old man's head turned to look in the direction of the nursery where Dean was playing. The old man then turned his head back toward Sue with what she described as an 'evil grin'.

Sue immediately dropped the bag of rubbish and ran into the house. She flew up the two flights of stairs and retrieved Dean from the nursery who was oblivious to the threat and seemed confused as to why his mom was acting so erratic. Sue recalls that on the way out of the house she noticed a freezing cold feeling that she seemed to run through as she passed the open door of the bedroom where the old man had been seen.

Of course, there was no sign of the old man and Sue ran out of the house, dragging Dean behind her to her car. She never returned again.

Funnily enough, the owners of the house never questioned why.

SHUFFLING LADY?
CHELMSLEY WOOD.

This tale comes from one of my aunts who is no longer with us. She was a no-nonsense type of woman and to be honest, the type of person I would have expected to disbelieve talk of the supernatural.

When my cousins, of which there were two boys and two girls, were living with my aunt. They lived in a three bedroomed house on Conway road, Chelmsley Wood, near Birmingham.

The house had become available and was more suited to the family having been in a smaller residence prior. Upon moving in, the family found several items which had been left by the previous tenant. One such item was a large old bible which would have been more suited to an old church. Not being particularly religious, my Aunt removed the bible from the house and could not recall what happened to it. It was likely thrown away with the rubbish.

Not long after this clear out, my aunt started to become bothered by activities during the night which initially did not concern her, but as it became more often, it began to annoy. She described how she felt the need to discuss what she believed was my cousin's night-time antics and enquired as to why they had been up out of bed so much during the night. None of my cousins admitted to the nightly disturbances and to be frank, had no idea what their mother was referring to.

As time went by, the minor bumps and creaks during the night became more defined to walking along the upstairs landing. To be precise, it was the sound of a step followed by a dragging noise repeated as though somebody was shuffling along the corridor to the last bedroom, upon reaching the door of this bedroom, the noise would then stop. It eventually got to the stage where all occupants were reporting the disturbances during the early hours, but no one was admitting to causing them.

As the noises continued, the whole household began to investigate to see exactly who was creating the disturbance. Whenever they occurred, they would quickly open the bedroom door to find out which one of them was shuffling along the landing. But no one was ever there. Even when the noises were right outside the door, when opened quickly, the landing would be empty.

The occurrences were enough for my aunt to discuss with other family members and even neighbours, which revealed a disturbing fact about the home's previous occupant. Immediately before my aunts family, an old lady had been resident in the house and was the only previous tenant from when the houses were built in the late 1960's. She was described as a deeply religious woman who had suffered ill health later in life while living on Conway road; having suffered a stroke during her old age. As a result of this, she had developed a weakness along one side of her body causing her to drag her one leg as she walked, hence making a shuffling noise. The old lady eventually died in the house and had been found dead on the landing.

Was the old lady looking for her bible which had been removed from the house?

WHERE TO GUVNOR? –
FEN END, WARKS.

When we were younger, my dad became a black cab driver, the following picture was taken with my younger brother in the back whilst my dad was polishing the outside. When the photo was processed, we noticed that a dark image, reminiscent of a humanlike shape appeared in the front driver's seat. At the time the picture was taken. Nobody was in the cab at the time.

Our family always get a chill from this picture.

LEAVE MY TOOLS ALONE. –
KNOWLE, SOLIHULL.

One of my job roles in the past was construction. I worked as a carpenter and a joiner and have sub-contracted for some larger building companies around Solihull and Birmingham.

Back in the late2000's, I found myself finishing a refurbishment job at a cottage in Knowle, Solihull. I had been on the project for a number of weeks as part of a team undertaking a significant refurbishment on the property which was in excess of 200 years old and within a stone's throw of the church.

As the job was nearly completed, I was now alone as I finished off what was known as snagging and remedials, which basically meant adjustments, minor repairs and addons.

It was very near to Christmas time at around 4pm, meaning it would have been dark and I would have needed to turn on the newly fitted lights in the old cottage. The task in hand was fitting some venetian style blinds, which would have been the last job before leaving site. I had set out each blind in the rooms they were to be fitted and worked my way around each one in turn. There were around four to be fitted.

On the first blind, I carefully measured out where the brackets were to be fitted and picked up my cordless drill to make a fixing hole. I approached where I had marked the hole and realised, I had not made enough of a mark with my pencil to be able to see in the poor light I had.

I put the drill down next to me and reached for my tape measure. It was not where I thought it had been put. After turning around, scouting the floor for my tape, I realised I did not have it. I checked my pockets and made sure I had not clipped it onto my waistband, I had not. I ventured down from the first floor where I was working out onto the street to my van to find another tape measure, I always keep a spare tape just in case one gets lost under a floor or the spring breaks inside. This tape was a luminous green colour and I clipped it to my belt on my waistband. I continued to fit the first blind without a problem and thought little of misplacing the original tape measure, as I often misplaced tools on jobs.

As I gathered up the few tools that I had been using, I continued on to the second window in another room and set my tools out on the floor around me. With my replacement tape measure, I set out the markings for the second blind. I reached down to where my drill had been, waving my hand expecting to touch it. I could not feel it so glanced down. It was not there. I grunted under my breath as I returned to the first room, expecting to find the drill as I could not have brought it through with me. The room was as empty. Totally bare as it had been left awaiting the customers furniture. I quickly scouted through the newly refurbished rooms, expecting to have put my wayward tools in one of them subconsciously, I did not find them.

Eventually returning to room 2 and feeling puzzled, I found the drill exactly where I had expected it to have been when ready to drill the second blind.

I muttered something about being stupid under my breath and managed to fit the second blind problem free. I still did not have the original tape measure at this point, but I thought little of it.

On the third room, I entered and immediately felt a chill like an icy blast run through me, so much so I thought the windows had been opened. But they had not, and I continued to mark out the blind. Again, I placed the tools on the floor immediately where I was working so they were in easy reach. I reached down to my waistband to grab my second tape measure and was exasperated to find it was not there.

I looked on the floor, I saw my cordless drill, pencil a screwdriver and a small packet of fixings for the blind. But no tape-measure. I turned around to the left and cast my eye across the floor space, 'nothing'. As I turned to the right, I heard a sliding noise across the floor, I again turned left and immediately spotted my tape measure. Not the bright green one, but my original yellow and black one that had gone missing in room one. I bent down and recovered the tape and looked at it momentarily.

At this point I really felt spooked and started to wonder what was going on. So much so that I walked around the entire site, checking for co-workers or any person that could have picked up my tools. The whole building was completely empty apart from me.

I felt very uneasy returning back up to the third room to fit blind three. I approached cautiously and entered the room. All my tools were there, and I had no problems whilst fitting blind three. In the last room I again started setting out the brackets for the blind and once again realised that both tape-measures were again missing.

In my frustration I called out "will you leave my tools alone?" as soon as I had said this, I heard a thump somewhere which sounded like was on the same floor but in another room.

I slowly walked out and headed toward the first room where I thought the noise had come from. As I arrived, I saw two tape-measures on the floor underneath the window where the first blind was fitted. It was both my black and yellow tape-measure and my luminous green one. I was surprised to find a small drill bit with them that I did not even realise had been missing.

I stood looking at the tools for a moment before calling out "thank you".

I left the cottage and have had no need to return. I sometimes drive past when driving through Knowle and glance up to the windows half expecting to see someone looking out at me laughing.

HOUSEWARMING, ELMDON, SOLIHULL.

This story was told to me in the 80's by the mom of a friend who I grew up with when I lived in Elmdon, near to Elmdon park, Solihull. For the story, her name is Mary.

My friend's parents had recently moved into the area and were hosting a housewarming party with several friends. This was in the late 1960's.

As the evening got late and most of the guests had left, only a handful of people remained at the party. At some point a Ouija board session was suggested. Now Ouija boards have always been frowned upon and most people would run a mile from the thought of playing with them.

On this occasion, those that did not want to dabble with the occult was outweighed by those that did. Mary reluctantly sat down at the table in the lounge along with her husband Jim and four remaining friends one of which was called Jane.

One of the other friends, Des, had drawn out a Ouija board made from a piece of card from a box used for the recent house move.

Des encouraged everyone to place a finger on an upturned glass used a planchette for the supposed spirit to point at each letter when answering the groups questions. Des took control of the session and was calling out the usual "Is anybody there?" type questions.

After much joking around and constantly trying to make each other jump, generally not taking any of it seriously, the glass began to move slowly.

The group watched in bewilderment as the glass landed on 'Hello'.

After each friend had accused each other of deliberately moving the glass, Des eventually asked who was there.

Slowly the makeshift planchette spelt out the name 'Albert'.

Some of the friends, Mary and Jane removed their hands from the glass, complaining that it was getting too frightening and wanted to stop. Des warned them to replace their fingers on the glass as the session would need to be closed properly. They reluctantly did and Des began the process of closing the session. Instead of responding to the 'goodbye' that Des had spoken in order to finish, the glass began to spell out another word.

Slowly the glass hovered over the letters "J – A – N – E".

Everybody looked towards Jane inquisitively, Janes eyes widened as she realised her name had been spelt out, all this time Des was repeating "don't let go!"

After a few moments, the makeshift planchette continued and spelt out "G-O, H – O – M – E"

Jane immediately leapt up, letting go of the glass, which did not move again.

She was visibly shaking and after trying to laugh it off, accusing the group of playing tricks, she left the party to return home.

Mary did not hear from her friend for a few days, and her telephone was either constantly engaged or just ringing out.

Eventually Des was able to update Mary and Jim on how Jane was doing.

Jane was well. Just terribly upset. After getting

home after the party she found out that her father had died from a heart attack.

What made it more compelling was that her dads name was Albert.

OLD FRIEND, HIGHFIELD ROAD, BIRMINGHAM.

This story comes from my mom and was told to her as occurred back in the late 1950's.

My mom's eldest sister Margaret and her husband at the time, Frank, had recently moved into a new home on Highfield road, Birmingham. Shortly before the move, the couple had received the tragic news that a close, male friend of theirs, Reg, had died suddenly.

Both Margaret and Frank were totally devastated by the loss of their friend in the prime of his life and had been on their minds constantly even whilst they made the move to their new home

Margaret always used to say to my mom that she could feel that Reg was around her although she never embellished on how these feelings emerged. Except for the following.

Having settled into their new home, all the furniture had been put in place and the smaller items within. Again, Margaret and

Frank had been reminiscing about their old friend and feeling quite low that he never got to see them in their new home. As they were recalling the departed friend, a large, heavy pine dresser that was right in front of them literally jumped away from the wall. Margaret and Frank were shocked at the ease in which the large item had been thrust away from the wall toward the centre of the room. Interestingly though, neither were scared at the incident and both believed it to be a sign from Reg.

From this point, they took comfort that Reg was around them and felt that he had in fact seen their new home. Although they never forgot him, there was never any other strange incidents reported in the home.

STRANGE HAPPENINGS,
DAMSON WOOD, SOLIHULL.

This story happened around 2006 and was told to my younger brother by his school friend. The events were actually caught on a camera phone at one time, but I have not been privy to them.

The friend, Sam, lived with his family at the time and was at senior school age. The family had lived in the home for some years with no reports of anything spooky going on, until one day, Sam had come from his upstairs bedroom one winter evening and crossed the landing, heading to go down the stairs for his evening dinner. As he crossed the landing, he felt a shadow cast across him and felt a cold shiver of air. This caused Sam to stop and look around the landing which was relatively small at about 6 by 3 or 4 feet. Instantly, Sam knew no one else was present as he paused to look around. The main landing light was on and he even had the forethought to look for a bug or moth around the light. There was none.

As he was about to move, he saw a full height,

human shaped, shadow dart across the wall, disappearing into a doorway to a bedroom. Sam immediately jumped down the stairs and ran to his family and blurted out what he had witnessed. The family were somewhat bewildered and spent some time investigating the landing area with nothing to be found, probably putting it down to the teenagers imagination.

A few weeks later, when the memory of what he had seen was fading, Sam was sat on his bed in his room, doing his homework. It was around the same time of day as before, it was dark outside and nearly teatime. This time. Sam did not need to go out onto the landing to feel the same fright that he now recalled weeks prior.

This time, it started with a scratching at the door, almost like a pet scratching to be let in, only the family had no pets. Eventually, Sam plucked up the courage to get up and approach the door slowly. As he held the door handle, he could feel the vibration of the scratching noises though his hand, with a deep breath he pulled the door open fast. He saw nothing.

As weeks went by, the noises became louder and even escalated into knocks and bangs during the night, usually when the family had been sleeping. The family also complained of witnessing shadows in the corners of their eyes. These occurrences continued for about three months. Then as suddenly as they started, they stopped. From what I am aware no occurrences had happened since.

FRIENDLY VISITOR? – FRANCIS ROAD, BIRMINGHAM.

During the early 1970's, my family lived on Francis road in Birmingham. My parents had been married only a few years, my older brother was a young child and I would have been only a couple of years old and recall nothing of this time myself. But my parents recall their experiences as follows.

It all started when they had not long moved in, my dad's sister in law was visiting for the first time with his brother and almost immediately appeared at unease. As she was shown around the new home, she became increasingly agitated and upon entering the front lounge, suddenly stopped and exclaimed that something strange had happened in the room. She went on to explain that something did not feel right in the new home and she could feel a presence.

Within only a few moments she had left and felt so uneasy that she did not visit this house again. As time went by, my parents had not really thought much of the remarks and were moving on with their lives, with nothing unusual to report. Until my older brother started coming back into the house after playing in the back garden with 'the man'.

My parents thought nothing much of my brothers claims and probably thought he had an imaginary friend.

Things became a little more concerning as time went on, such as one day, my mom heard a knock at the door and went to answer it. As she opened the door she was met by a quite unremarkable, middle-aged woman who immediately brushed past my mom into our home. My mom, who was dumbstruck by this, followed the woman as she manoeuvred around the ground floor of the property.

Eventually, the woman stopped in the front lounge where my aunt had complained of an uneasy presence. Standing still for a short while, the woman gazed at a single armchair in the lounge, this chair had been left in the house when my parents brought the house and seemed in good order, so was kept.

After pausing for what seemed like a while,

the woman blurted out "My husband died in that chair!"

My mom was speechless and before she could even think of a reply to the statement, the woman had left the room and was leaving the house. The woman was never seen by my mom again.

At around the same time, my brothers play mate, the man from the garden, was now playing with him in his bedroom on a regular basis. This together with my brothers noticeably young affiliation with matches and one serious wardrobe fire which was bad enough for the local fire service to be called. Fortunately, no one was hurt.

My mom recalls having put my brother and me to bed one night, she went about her daily duties and found herself washing up after preparing dinner in the kitchen.

Without warning she describes feeling a forceful prod in her back, almost causing her to drop the item she was washing up. Turning around ready to tell off my older brother for hitting her back she was astonished to find no one there. She was bewildered at how my brother could have escaped the large open kitchen so quickly without being seen and immediately went in search of him.

Almost straight away she realised that both my brother and I were sound asleep in bed and she was on her own in the house. My dad had been at work at the time.

During their time at Francis road, my family felt an unease and had issues with pungent smells that used to appear from nowhere specific with no apparent causes.

They were very happy to have moved on from this address when they eventually did.

MUSICAL MANIFESTATION, BIRMINGHAM.

The following story was told to me in the mid 1990's by a police sergeant who it had happened to.

The officer, Ray, who at the time of the incident was a constable, had been called to a suspected burglary at a primary school near Birmingham. The police had been alerted via a silent alarm system which meant the police knew that someone or something had triggered a sensor on the premises although, an alarm was not sounding at the school itself.

The police officer arrived at the school and began to circle around the building looking for signs of entry. The school was in total darkness and everywhere was silent. Eventually he found an open window which was just big enough to fit through. At the time he wondered why the window did not seem to have been forced open, he queried if it had simply been left open, as after all, it was summer time and they had been in the middle of a particularly warm spell and maybe someone had forgot to close it at the end of the day. Ray quietly contacted the police control room of what he had found using his radio, before carefully climbing into the open window finding himself in a classroom.

As he ventured toward the classroom door and out onto a corridor, he stood still, momentarily holding his breath as he could hear a faint sound which appeared to be coming from one end of the long, dark corridor.

Ray pointed his police issue torch along the long walkway and saw nothing of interest as he proceeded down the darkness. As he did so, the noise became louder and realised it was music of some kind. As he neared the source of the music, Ray realised the sound was that of a piano being played. He likened the music to be that of a hymn of sorts, exactly the type that would not be out of place in a school assembly. As he neared the end of the long corridor, he found he was standing at a set of double doors which had been left open. The doors were indeed the entrance to the school's assembly hall.

Ray cautiously entered the large hall, all the

time the music played. The large hall was pitch black except for the dim green 'exit' lights which barely illuminated above each exit door around the hall.

He cast his torch to where the sound seemed to be coming from and found a dark wooden piano in the far corner of the room. Ray stealthily approached the large instrument in order to get a view of the far side of the piano to see who would be sat at the keyboard which was still being played.

As he arrived at the piano and was within only a few feet of the stool which was perched in front of the black and white keys, he realised there was no one there. Coincidentally, as he made this realisation, the music immediately stopped playing leaving an echo of the last chord played to resonate around the room before an eery silence was left.

Eventually the officer was joined by another police colleague and the school's caretaker who after checking the alarm system could confirm that the assembly hall had been the only sensor to have been triggered. The rest of the building had been secure, and no property had been removed.

Although physically shaken at the time, Ray confessed that he did not discuss what he had found for many months. To this day he had no idea what had caused the piano music to be played and that no rational reason seemed to fit.

SCHOOL REVISITED, BIRMINGHAM.

As a police officer myself in the 1990's, I discussed the previous story with Ray. It had arisen after I had indeed attended the same school for the same reason. I did not find a self-playing piano, but I did find that the school had been burgled. Offenders had actually forced entry into the school but for some reason had not removed any property. We waited for the caretaker to arrive so the school could be secured.

The caretaker told us that the alarm system had been downgraded because it always seemed to go off for no apparent reason. Engineers believed that the reason must have been due to insects or bugs being detected by the sensors and after numerous attempts at adjusting them, they simply disarmed the troublesome areas.

We discussed the fact that entry had been gained on this occasion as a back window to the schools computer room was forced open and had caused considerable mess and damage, we had also found a number of foot-prints leading us to believe that at least two people had been involved. We could not work out why several small items had been moved to the window, but nothing appeared to have been removed from the school. The caretaker was not as surprised as we were and continued to tell us of some interesting tales which he had witnessed after hours in the school

It seemed that the caretaker was aware of the spooky past at the school and recalled numerous times that he had been followed around the school after hours by an unseen force which continually whistled old fashioned tunes. On some occasions he said he felt that the whistling was right next to him and that cleaners and some other staff had experienced the same type of incident.

The caretaker also recounted a more sinister episode where he was walking along the long corridor at night, checking the doors to each room off it. Having reached the end of the corridor he turned and caught sight of a figure standing at the opposite end.

As he focused on the figure which he described

as a light grey wispy figure, he described that it appeared blurred and could not quite focus on it. Before he knew what was happening, he noticed that the figure appeared to fade out below the legs and that whatever it was, had started gliding the length of the corridor towards him at speed.

The caretaker ran out of the building quickly and for some time would not go into the school on his own.

Before my conversation with the caretaker ended, he recalled the incident that Ray had attended and recalled that although Ray did not admit to seeing something that night, he could tell by the look on his face that something had occurred.

This was backed up by the fact that for some reason Ray continued to point his torch around the building even when all the lights had been turned on.

NEW STREET STATION, BIRMINGHAM.

Birmingham`s largest railway station was originally planned in 1846 and subsequently opened to passengers in 1851. Since this time there have been many renovations and upgrades. Over the years, many people have believed the station to be haunted.

One such haunting is that of an old train driver who is reported to have taken his own life in the waiting room on platform four. Since then, his ghost or at least a figure of a man in uniform is said to be seen around platform four re-enacting his final moments up until his suicide.

This was not the only reported suicide at New street station, in fact there are reports of no less than four suicides here. Another man, reputedly called Claude, who took his own life around the

turn of the 20th century has been seen by commuters using the hub. Claude is said to be very recognisable in his Victorian attire.

The station has been involved in several incidents over the years and has required major reconstruction.

In the 1920's, two trains collided leaving at least 3 people dead and numerous injured. During the second world war, the station suffered significant bomb damage and again required refurbishment.

Right from the original construction, many people believed New street station to be cursed, this was because in 1848 a graveyard was dug up and moved to make way for the station.

If you visit platform four, you might see more than you expect to.

FARM SIGHTING, BALSALL COMMON.

Back in the early 1980's, an old friend of mine had the following occurrence that has stayed with her all her life since. Her name is Jess and at the time she was 13 years old and lived with her family on their farm near Balsall common, in rural Solihull.

It was the middle of the summer holidays and she was just waking up as the sun was streaming through the thin curtains of her ground floor bedroom window.

As she came around from her sleep, she became aware that she could make out a silhouette of a man on her curtain. This was not disturbing to her as It would not be unusual for another member of the family to be at the back of the bungalow or even one of the farm workers, although she recalled it may have been a little early. In order to check, she sprung onto her knees at the end of her bed and pulled the curtain back. As soon as she did, she was delighted to see her grandad standing outside. It had been a nice surprise as her grandad did not live on the farm but was a couple of miles away. He would regularly pop by to see his son, daughter in law and grandchildren and check on the farm from which he was now retired. Jess recalled he was wearing the all in one blue overall's that he would wear when occasionally helping her dad on the farm.

Jess opened up her bedroom window and called out to her grandad. The old man seemingly did not hear his granddaughter and had started walking away toward the side of the bungalow. Jess leapt out of bed and ran into the family lounge just in time to see her grandad again through the large patio doors. The old man was looking straight ahead so did not make eye contact with Jess or even look towards the house. This made Jess uncomfortable as her grandad was usually a very cheery type who would normally be alert to Jess' presence.

Her grandad continued walking on in the direction of the front of the house, so Jess ran to the front door. She opened the door onto the large farmyard and immediately saw her mom and dad getting out of the family car. Her parents glanced at each other before her dad approached and hugged her into his body.

He then continued to tell Jess the devastating news that her grandad had died during the night. Jess became very confused as she ran around the side of the family home expecting to see her grandad.

He was nowhere to be seen, leaving her even more frustrated. She was dumbstruck by the news her dad had delivered and it was a while before she was able to discuss what she had seen with her family.

Eventually Jess came to terms with her grandfather's death and likes to think that seeing him was his way of letting her know he had gone or was saying goodbye.

SOLIHULL AMBULANCE
STATION, SOLIHULL.

The old ambulance station on Hermitage road was used as an ambulance hub from the mid 1960`s. It was reportedly haunted by a ghost in an old services uniform believed to have been from the air force. Other stories state the man was a soldier who died in the nearby Hermitage which is an old Victorian house adjacent to the station's grounds.

Before it closed in 2013, The ambulance service ran numerous responding ambulances from Solihull and many of the staff reported strange happenings around the building.

Many of the staff were aware of strange occurrences in the station from creaks and bumps, to movements in the corner of their eyes. On some occasions the main doors used to be knocked only for no one to be there.

I recall speaking to a maintenance assistant for the ambulance station, Clive before it was closed down, he was well aware of the stories of the strange happenings and claims to have seen a figure of a man in old fashioned military style uniform around the stores area on numerous occasions.

The stores were at the very back of the building nearer to the old Hermitage. He also recalled feeling that someone was watching him from that area as he would clean ambulances knowing he was in the building on his own.

On another occasion a member of staff said they could hear a female voice repeating "yoo-hoo" and "Hello" as if to get their attention along the hallway between the station officers office and the main crew room. Upon inspection, no one could be found, and the paramedic found they were all alone in the building. These calls have been heard by numerous members of staff at different times of day and night.

Some unconfirmed stories tell of a man many years ago who had reportedly taken his own life by hanging himself in the building or on the site where the ambulance station stood.

The building still stands on Hermitage road and is still used as some kind of community centre.

MARSTON GREEN HOSPITAL
SITE, MARSTON GREEN.

Just off Berwicks lane where Marston Green meets Chelmsley Wood lies a relatively new housing estate where Marston Green Hospital once stood.

Before its closure and subsequent demolition, the hospital was formerly a maternity hospital. Prior to this, it was a military hospital for the Canadian services built prior to the second world war. The housing estate was built in the early 1990's and has had several reports of strange and even some distressing supernatural activity.

Having lived in a cul de sac on the estate, between 1994 and 2001, I can recall some strange and disturbing things in our home during this time.

At the time I was a police officer and I worked alternative days or nights, leaving my wife at home alone during the night quite often.

One day having been on a night shift, I awoke around late morning and went downstairs to spend time with my wife. As we caught up the previous few days, I was surprised at the next question my wife asked me. She asked what had caused me to come home during my night shift.

I paused for a while before confirming that I had not actually been home during the night.

My wife confirmed that at around two o`clock in the morning, she was awoken after hearing our front door unlatch, followed by footsteps climbing the stairs. this was followed with what she described as rummaging around upstairs before the footsteps were again heard descending the stairs before the front door was closed. She had been expecting me to put my head around the bedroom door to check in on her as I normally would if I had popped home to use the facilities. All of this had happened within a few moments and she was certain she had not dreamt it.

This incident seemed to be a precursor to a barrage of activity at this address which lasted until we started a family and we eventually moved out.

The next report of activity was when we were both at home in the living room, watching television one evening. As we sat, relaxed with our feet up, we both suddenly looked at each other as we followed a series of footsteps across the ceiling, indicating that someone was walking across our bedroom. I immediately ran up to the bedroom as the footsteps were so real that I was certain that somebody was in there. The room was empty, and nothing was out of place. This was quite an alarming issue and recalling the previous issue we started suspecting something was not quite right with the house. We dismissed it for the time being as it could have been settlement of the new building and the fact it *was* a new building.

These footsteps happened a lot and became a talking point around the family, we often tried to rationalise them until one day I spoke with my next-door neighbour whose house was adjoined on the living room wall side.

One day I was out the front, washing our car, as was Melvin from next door. Melvin was a no-nonsense Yorkshire man in his 60's. He was quite brash and was not frightened to speak his mind. I would have assumed he would not be the type to be affected by stories of the supernatural or believe them for that matter.

As I continued throwing a soapy sponge at my

car, I heard Mel call over to me.

"Hey Neil, can I ask you a serious question?" He asked, seeming somewhat sheepish.

I approached Mel with an inquisitive look and assured him he could.

With a little hesitation Mel said, "have you had anything strange happen in your house?"

This was surprising to me although somewhat relieving, without giving anything away I answered, "what like?"

Mel then went on to explain how he had been suffering remarkably similar happenings to what we had and in fact his were far worse.

I listened with interest how he and his wife had encountered the same footsteps in his bedroom that disappeared at the wall between our two adjoining properties. I worked out that where the footsteps finished on his side, they would continue on ours, as we had witnessed.

I felt that I put Mel out of his misery when I

told him that we had suffered the same type of unexplainable activity. This seemed to spur him on to continue with more information about what was going on next door. He continued to tell me how his wife had seen the figure of a man standing in the doorway to the bedroom who appeared to be watching them sleep, Mel had rubbished the sighting until he himself had witnessed the dark figure himself some evenings later. The activity still escalated more. Mel described how both his wife and he had been awoken one night to a tapping noise only to then hear a loud crash which turned out to be a mirror smashing on the floor in the hallway which had previously fixed directly to the wall.

Mel agreed that prior to these incidents he had no belief in anything supernatural, but he was now believing something was happening.

I told him of our experiences which at the time seemed very minor compared to his. As we parted, we agreed to keep each other updated with what was going on.

On the opposite side we had another neighbour, Shelly, who was close to my wife.

Shelly was a scientist working for a large company in Birmingham developing coatings for metal containers and when my wife broached the subject of whether she had experienced anything unusual, Shelly replied with a categorical no and that she did not believe in such things.

Within only a matter of weeks, we had loud knocking on our door to find Shelly in an emotional mess having seen the shadow of a figure in her house which moved and disappeared as she watched it. She was unable to rationalise the incident and as such it had frightened her enormously.

Shelly also continued to experience further happenings which forced her to eventually move out soon after. The house was then occupied by an elderly lady and her grown up son.

Some time passed, we were still having strange bangs and footsteps around the home, but nothing more than this. We had been made aware that the whole croft had been suffering a significant amount of bad luck and hardship.

Of the twenty houses and in a relatively short

time in the croft, there had been a sudden death of someone who became alcohol dependant since moving in, a cot death of a child, two heart attacks, one which was my next door neighbour Mel, numerous family break ups and even one of our neighbours died mysteriously while on holiday. We were also aware of two of our more elderly neighbours developing cancer in the croft.

In 1997, we were expecting our first child, when my wife was about 7 months pregnant, we came home from shopping just as it was getting dark. I opened the front door and felt inside for the light switch. Just as I was about to flick the switch, I realised a pungent smell emitting from inside the house and quickly realised the whole house was full of gas. I entered the house and quickly saw that all the switches on our gas cooker in the kitchen had been turned on.

This was a really frightening experience, had I not realised the gas was on, the whole house (and neighbours) could have been destroyed taking us with it. I could find no evidence of anybody gaining access to our home unless they had acquired a key. This incident was difficult to put down to a supernatural experience and we were seriously concerned about our safety there.

Only a couple of months after this incident, our first child was due when my wife unexpectedly suffered a serious haemorrhage whilst at home. She was rushed by ambulance into hospital and thankfully both my wife and my first son were saved. My son has suffered a lifelong brain injury as a result, but I am thankful I have them both and he has a good life.

The activities around the croft continued and we were aware that the elderly neighbour next door had been complaining of strange people in her house on a daily basis, I had been called around by her son one day who was a quiet chap who seemed very shy and was on the autistic spectrum, his mother had been particularly upset at some strange happenings and he did not know where to turn. While I was in their kitchen, I witnessed a lid from a sugar pot slide across the counter. Even with what had been going on for the past few years I could not believe what I had seen and still question it to this day. The old lady eventually moved to a care home and her son moved away.

Eventually, we moved away from this cul de sac. I am not aware of what is happening there to this day, but I was made aware that Mel had suffered a further heart attack and died at home. I also came across one of the elderly residents from the croft who had developed cancer when living in the croft. He explained how he had made a full recovery when he and his wife moved away. I have not been back to this croft since and I have no plans to go back.

A CARE HOME IN TILE CROSS, BIRMINGHAM.

Quite often, my work in the ambulance service would have taken me around many care and nursing homes. I would meet old men and woman with great stories to tell, and also nursing and care staff. One particular occasion, I met a woman who cared for the elderly at a care home in Tile Cross, Birmingham.

It was another gloomy, dull, Autumnal day and the carer was escorting a female patient into hospital. It must have been around the end of October, as the main entrance to the care home had Halloween decorations around the front entrance.

In passing I must have asked what, if any plans they had for the residents for Halloween and the carer responded that the care home was spooky enough without Halloween. This certainly sparked my interest and the carer continued to tell the following.

It had always been fairly common knowledge

between some of the staff that the home had some strange occurrences. Some areas of the large building, which was attached to another care facility next door, made this carer nervous.

She had not spotted anything to cause concern herself but was able to recall numerous residents that had seen an entity on many occasions. The carer recalled one evening helping an elderly resident, Jean, get ready for bed. As she helped her to disrobe, they chatted and passed the time of day. Jean may have needed physical assistance, but her mind was still a sharp as a younger woman.

At some point during helping the resident, she noticed the resident had stopped talking. She noticed that Jean's gaze appeared to be fixed on something behind her. She turned around and with not seeing anything specific asked Jean what she was looking at. Jean looked puzzled before she said she had been looking at a young boy standing behind the carer. She added that the boy, aged around 5, had appeared and was staring back at her before walking away.

Although the carer had not seen the boy,

she described feeling a cold wave wash over her which physically made her shudder. After briefly checking the room and then the corridor outside, no outside visitors could be found at that time.

The little boy has been seen around the care home on numerous occasions by residents, he does not speak or make any sound. He has been described as wearing 1960's or 70's style clothing. He is usually accompanied by a sudden drop in temperature.

No one can be certain where the child comes from or what the exact history may be but the carer was certain that a public house once stood where the care home is and that a child had been tragically killed in a fire in the upstairs, residential area of the pub some years before.

SHELDON HALL, TILE CROSS.

During the late 1970's, my family spent a short time living in Kingshurst, just outside Birmingham. I spent much of my play time around Babbs Mill lake and Kingshurst park.

Just over the border into Tile cross from the park stood a near-derelict building, Sheldon hall, which at the time we called Baldies mansion.

The large house had a history dating back to the 16th century but had become abandoned in the early 1900`s and fallen into disrepair. This made it a hive of attention for the local kids and many spooky stories were born from the old manor house.

One such story came from a friend who lived locally to me. David was about 14 at the time and like me spent much of his childhood playing around the lake and exploring the dilapidated hall. He reports that he had been venturing around the overgrown grounds of the hall one evening with his brother, Steven, and another friend Jason. They had been rummaging around as kids do and generally exploring.

David told me the following.

They had been walking around the old building and trying to peer through some of the boards put up on the windows to see what they could see and daring each other to go inside.

As they ventured around, they noticed a light emitting from inside the house. Initially they stopped in their tracks not knowing who was responsible for the light, which appeared to be moving around the ground floor of the property. Eventually, David, who was the more daring of the trio, approached a window. He peered through a gap in a board which was fixed across the stone framed aperture. After shifting his head from side to side in order to get a better view of the inside of the property, David suddenly jumped back from the window and began running back in the direction of the lake. Not knowing what had caused this reaction, he was followed quickly by Steven and Jason. Eventually the three regrouped well away from the mansion and David explained why he had fled.

Initially he saw the light in the building and thought it was a torch and expected to see other kids exploring the abandoned property. Eventually the source of the light became apparent and he saw a woman holding a candle stick. The woman was wearing old fashioned clothing but appeared to have some sort of material over her head which David described amusingly as a white 'tea towel', it seemed that the figure was looking for something a she appeared to be turning her head and looking left and right. David explained that what caused him to flee was when the figure looked directly toward the youth and seemed to fix her gaze on him.

This story fits well with some of the local tales of Sheldon Hall. Some stories tell of a former wife of a farmer who was murdered in the hall who is reputed to walk the old building searching for her murderer. She is described as wearing period dress with a ruff or Elizabethan collar. There is no mention of a tea towel though, although a masked figure has been seen around the grounds.

Many of the local kids claim to have seen lights in and around the building and I even saw some lights myself on one of the occasions I found myself playing with friends on the grounds. It had been quite late on the evening and was dark and from what I recall, we could all see a dim light coming from the around some of the boards on the window. None of us were brave enough to approach the building to investigate the origin of the light.

In the 1990's, plans were made to demolish the old hall but instead it was saved and became a restaurant. Other stories have since evolved.

People have claimed that figures have appeared on photographs in and around the property. Staff members report seeing the old lady and also the ghost of a little girl to this day.

BALDWINS LANE, HALL GREEN.

In the 1990's, A former work friend Adam, rented a house on Baldwins lane in Hall Green, Birmingham with his friend Rick. The house was a large three bed semi-detached house, which was perfect for him and his dog Bruno, a Golden Retriever. Adam had known Rick since school and they were good friends, Adam was the main tenant, with Rick renting a room from him and paying a contribution for food and utility bills. The location was good for Adam's work and he knew the area really well as he had grown up on the adjoining Scribers lane, in fact his parents were still there so he could visit any time and they could pop in to feed the dog when he was at work.

On moving in day, Adam and his friend, Rick had hired a van and moved all of the furniture in themselves. The last thing that Adam needed to do was to pick up Bruno from his parent's house around the corner and walk him round.

As he walked his dog along the garden path

to his new home, Adam realised that Bruno was pulling against his lead, seemingly reluctant to approach the house. Adam gently persuaded the dog in and gave him a reassuring pat before the dog slipped under the kitchen table and lay down. Rick could be heard banging around upstairs, sorting out his furniture. Adam called up to him offering a hot drink as Adam was putting the kettle on. Due to the banging around and shuffling of furniture, Rick did not respond so Adam assumed he was busy and left him to it.

Eventually Adam fell into an armchair in the living room and dropped his feet onto one of the remaining boxes full of personal belongings. As he sipped his coffee and relaxed back into the chair, the noises coming from the upstairs reduced before soon stopping all together. Adam finished his coffee thinking about what he could have for his tea, just as he heard a rattling noise coming from the front door. Wondering what the noise was, he jumped to his feet and entered the hallway. He approached the front door just as his housemate Rick was coming into the house. Rick was holding a large brown paper package under his arm and mentioned he had picked up fish and chips for them both. As he passed

Adam, he dropped the package of food onto the kitchen worktop.

Adam stared as Rick continued to search through the kitchen drawers looking for cutlery, eventually he noticed Adams stare and queried what was wrong. Adam informed his friend that he had heard somebody banging around upstairs and presumed it had been Rick and was now wondering who had been up there.

Both men ran up the stairs and began to look through each of the rooms. Nothing had seemed out of place from how they had both left them and it actually occurred to Adam that the fairly lightweight furniture would not really have caused the amount of noise he had heard.

This was one of many strange occurrences that both Adam and Rick experienced in the home. The dog seemed so distressed in the property and constantly whimpered and growled that he moved permanently to Adam's parent's house where he settled to his normal self immediately.

Bumps and sounds of furniture scrapings were heard at all times of the day and night by both Adam and Rick, with no cause to be found.

One day, about six weeks after moving in, Adam had already left for work for the day and Rick was about to do the same. He left the house and walked a short distance before he got on a bus at the end of the road. Rick took a seat on the upper deck before looking out of the window. As he looked out, the bus was passing his house and Rick stared across at the property.

He was horrified as he saw an old white-haired man wearing dark glasses staring out of 'his' bedroom window at him. The old mans gaze was fixed on Ricks and followed him as the bus passed the house. Rick ran down to the bus driver and asked him to stop the bus, luckily the driver did, and Rick ran back to the property. The old man was nowhere to be seen both from outside and inside the house, equally there was no sign of any entry or disturbance.

After months of unusual happenings and disturbing occurrences, Rick moved out which caused a bit of bad feeling between the friends, as Adam was left to cover the living costs alone and he felt worried about being in the house alone. After managing to get to the agreed six months on the rental contract, the noises and unusual happenings had continued so Adam did not renew the lease and moved back in with his parents.

As time passed and Rick and Adam re-acquainted and began to socialise again. One evening they met up at Adams parents house on Scribers lane with plans to walk to the local Baldwins pub. As they walked, they reminisced about the strange happenings that had occurred at the house on Baldwins lane. As they did, they realised they had been passing the house and were stood on the opposite side of the road from the house. They could see a letting agent sign in the garden and Adam remarked that it always seemed up for rent and no one seemed to stay there for very long. As they continued to look, both men simultaneously noticed somebody watching them from the upstairs bedroom window. It was the same old man with white hair wearing the glasses that Rick had seen, looking right at them.

Both men ran to the pub and actually laughed

about it after but neither of them would look at the house again and tried to avoid passing it when they could.

CHELMSLEY WOOD
SHOPPING CENTRE.

Opened in 1970, Chelmsley wood shopping centre has had its share of ghost stories over the years. The following story has been told to me by a former worker at a shoe shop on the town centre and happened during the 1980`s. The woman, who I will call Sally, had not long been working at the store and was settling into the role well. Her role included serving customers in the main shop and collecting shoes which were stored in the main storeroom situated directly underneath, the same as most of the shops on the shopping centre.

On this particular occasion, the day had been drawing to a close and she had been asked to tidy the main storeroom as during the day shoes tended to be put back in the wrong places and needed to be put back in order.

As she was rearranging the stock, she saw her supervisor walk between the shoe racks and disappear back towards the stairs up to the main shop and assumed a customer had come in and was being fitted for shoes. After a little while Sally had put most of the stock in order and returned to the shop. She approached her supervisor and asked if she had sold the shoes she had been down for or if they needed to be returned to the store. Her supervisor looked puzzled for a moment and told Sally that they had not had a customer and that she had not been down to the store room as she could not have left the shop as they were the only staff remaining on site. The supervisor had been cashing up the till. With a smile, the she added that Sally had probably seen the ghost.

Sally`s puzzled look became that of shock as her colleague continued to tell her about a ghostly figure that was regularly seen by staff of the shoe shop, so much so that many of them became too frightened to stay. Others had reported freezing cold spells when it had been warm immediately before and the store-room lights being turned off leaving them in pitch-black, darkness. On some occasions a pale figure had been seen gliding between the racking. When the apparition was confronted, it would simply vanish.

Sally was made of sturdy stuff and whilst she worked at the shop encountered the presence on numerous occasions. She said she would talk to the entity when down in the store-room which she felt helped her to remain calm. She never heard of the origins of the ghost or the story behind who it may be, but never really felt threatened by it.

MONKSPATH, SOLIHULL.

There are many tales about how Monkspath in Solihull came to be named. I have heard that it had something to do with the route a monk or monks used to take when travelling through Solihull many years ago. Officially the name is reported to have come from the 12th century when the Earl of Warwick gave the land to Roger de Ulehale (of Tanworth) when the name was recorded as Munchespath. But I cannot confirm the actual origins for why it is called this. The following tales are a good enough reason for me.

There have been numerous sightings of a single hooded monk at various locations between Henley in Arden, all the way through to St Alphege church in Solihull town centre.

The following tales are the most compelling.

An older couple were out for a late walk in Hillfield park, after a large meal. As they neared the end of the park toward the main

Monkspath Hall road, they both spotted a figure that was totally covered in a brown cloak. Due to the late hour they thought it strange that anyone else would be out and about, let alone in such attire.

As they watched they realised that the figure appeared to glide along the road and that his lower legs disappeared into the ground. They watched the figure glide for a few moments until it vanished in some nearby bushes. The couple quickly headed home trying to make sense of what they had encountered.

Other accounts have told of a dark hooded figure closer to Solihull town centre around the area of Church Hill road.

The figure is often seen slowly gliding towards the church before simply vanishing in front of the viewer without making a sound.

CHESTER ROAD, ERDINGTON.

Numerous reports have arisen about a mysterious figure that appears on the Chester road, Erdington at the junction of the Tyburn road. The figure is said to suddenly appear before vanishing into thin air in front of the viewers eyes. One such story is that a nurse who worked at the nearby Good Hope hospital had rested momentarily at a bench. Then upon recouping and starting to move on had witnessed a misty apparition form in front of her, lasting for only a short time, the figure dissolved as quickly as it had appeared.

There is little evidence as to what the figure relates to, but local folklore mentions two possibilities. One being a local disabled boy who was murdered and subsequently decapitated by a soldier in the 18th century. His body was dumped in the nearby park at Pipe Hayes, whereas his head was removed and never found.

The second story is that the figure is a young girl called Mary who was murdered by a farmer's son after a dance in the early 19th century.

The figure is said to have appeared due to the man being found not guilty for the crime although the local community believed there was enough evidence to prove his guilt.

The bench near to where this sighting has occurred is said to hold dark feelings to some people when they rest there. Some people have felt low and depressed and describe a deep sadness come over at this location.

Story's from outside of the West Midlands

IRISH TALE, CO CORK.

Another former colleague from the ambulance service who is sadly no longer with us, told me the following story one day.

John had been visiting his sister who lived in a small cottage just outside Cork, Ireland.

Having arrived at his sister's cottage quite late on the evening, due to his travel plans not quite going as expected, he was ushered through to the kitchen where he was fed with soup and a glass of Guinness.

The kitchen was dimly lit, and the main source of light was the flames from the open fire in the dining area of the kitchen. John, having already partaken in drinking sessions along his prolonged travels from Birmingham to Ireland was self admittedly worse for wear. He recalls being shown to the cottages spare room. His bed had been made and John flopped onto it, needing to rest after the long day he had endured.

Before he dropped off, he thought he saw a

black shadow slowly swaying in the corner of the room. He considered it to be cast be the candle-light and he confessed he was in no shape to concern himself with this and in no time at all was fast asleep.

The following day he spent with his sister, catching up and sightseeing around the local area. His sister had arranged a meal at home in the cottage on the evening.

As the evening set in, John recalled that although his sister's cottage had all mod cons, she preferred candle-light and the light from the open fire. It was around 5pm on the evening and it was already dark outside, so the already fully roaring fire was welcome.

John's brother in law returned home from work and they all sat down at the dining table to eat. Following a heavy meal, john recalled how they retired into the main room in the cottage where the open fire with a few candles were dotted around gave a nice ambient light. A short while later, John was settled into a deep armchair and although tired from the large dinner he had consumed swore that he was alert and had not touched an alcoholic drink since the previous night.

His eyes were attracted to a shadow on the wall around the fireplace. With an inquisitive stare, he watched the shadow. It was sort of person shaped but initially remained still and he immediately recalled the shadow from the first night in his room.

Just as John was rationalising the shape on the wall, it moved. John jumped.

Johns sister and brother in law laughed as John stood up and watched the shadow disappear into an old doorway which in years gone by would have been to another room of the cottage but was now the cottage next door.

John, still standing with a startled look on his face turned to his sister. His sister explained that these shadows were a very regular occurrence in the cottage and that they were harmless.

It took John a few days to become used to these shadows, but eventually he did. He did however add that the swaying shadow in his room, even without the candle being lit, that watched him sleeping made him uncomfortable.

ALCATRAZ, SAN FRANCISCO.

As I said in the introduction, some of the stories are overseas. In 2004, my younger brother went on holiday to various locations around the USA. One of the stops found him in San Francisco where he was lucky enough to visit the old prison on the small island known as Alcatraz.

During the trip, he was able to walk around the old Alcatraz prison and explored old cells. All the time he was taking photographs.

When he returned home and was able to view the pictures on a computer monitor, he found the following image.

The picture was taken from inside a cell which had a reputation for strange happenings and sensations. It shows what appears to be two transparent legs with old fashioned styled footwear, not dissimilar to that of inmates that may have been housed in the prison's walls. Some people have argued that the picture is simply double exposure, but it was taken on a digital camera which would rule out this type of issue.

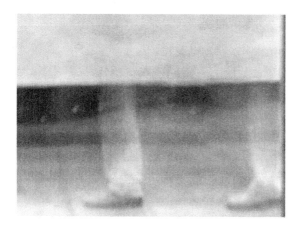

EYE FIDGET - ILFRACOMBE, DEVON.

During a break to Devon with my wife and my two sons in 2009, we stayed in a lovely, large guest house just outside Ilfracombe.

On the second night, I was awoken by the strangest sensation. I felt like someone was picking at my eyes trying to open them. Much like my children used to do when they were much younger, around toddler age. I found myself wide awake at around 3 o'clock in the morning. My family were all fast asleep and the whole guesthouse was silent. I ventured out to the kitchenette area of our suite, whilst feeling as though some small fingers had actually been plucking at my eye lids.

I poured myself a glass of water before making my way back to the bedroom. As I passed the main door, my attention was drawn to a giggling come from the other side of the door. I paused to hear more clearly and again heard what I would describe as a young girl giggling. I quietly opened the door and peeped out a small gap into the hall expecting to see someone across the large hall of the Victorian house. There was nothing to be seen, for that matter I heard nothing else either. I waited a few moments but nothing. Eventually, only slightly puzzled, I fell back to sleep.

Later that morning, the family went down for breakfast. Our over the table conversation turned to the unusual happenings I had felt and heard during the night. I asked our host (who was also serving us) about what other children were currently guests at the premises. She looked puzzled for a moment before stating that they were only two suites occupied at the time. My family and an older couple with no children. Our host did not really add much more but I was surprised when I came across the hosts husband who waited until I was alone before he spoke to me.

He mentioned about me asking about children around the guest house and proudly stated that he thought I had encountered the resident ghost. The house had been built in the late 18 hundreds and was a home to a family which included a young female child who had died in a tragic fall down the main staircase when aged four.

The young child had since been heard giggling

and had even been glanced on the odd occasion. The proprietor also told me that other residents had reported having their eye-lids gently touched when sleeping just as if a small child was trying to wake them up.

For the rest of the week, I was extra vigilant but saw or heard, 'or felt' no further from the apparition.

HAUNTED HOUSE VISIT, YORK.

In October of 2010 I stayed in York with my wife for a short break. Amongst other site seeing tours we looked around the 'Haunted house of York' attraction which is situated along Stonegate.

We have always had a curiosity with the supernatural and ghosts, so we were looking forward to it, although we did not know exactly what to expect.

The building is reported as being around 700 years old, so just looking around and taking in the history was also an interesting prospect.

We were put in a small group of people as we were prepared to start the tour. Our group consisted of a young family, Young man with a white hat, his partner a young blonde lady and their two boys aged around 8 to 10. Another young couple in their 20's and my wife and me.

Having entered the building at street level, as a group, we were ushered through to different rooms, up old narrow stairs, down even more narrow and creaking stairs, directed via pre-recorded audio messages which told of the varying historical events attached to the house.

I must add that except when we were moving between rooms, the house was in pitch darkness whilst stories relating to that particular room were told.

I had taken my digital camera with me and had been snapping pictures of some of the old rooms, using the flash to light up the surrounding darkness every now and then.

Eventually we finished off in a below street level basement, which was more like a storeroom full of old junk and a few items of furniture.

Like the other rooms, I snapped a couple of pictures of the basement and thought nothing of it. There were no incidents or reports of spooky noises or visions and having finished the tour we found a pub just off 'The Shambles' to have some lunch.

As we waited for our food to arrive, I decided to have a look through the photographs which I had taken on the haunted house tour.

As I swiped through the pictures on my digital camera to the basement photographs, my attention was drawn to something that I felt was out of place in one picture.

The picture was of an old glass fronted cabinet with mirrors along the back which was positioned along the outer wall of the basement.

In the reflection of the mirror glass of the cabinet, I could see a reflection of the young father with the white cap with one of his sons. I could also see a grainy reflection of somebody else, someone who was not part of our group.

The reflection appears to show an older man with a grey cap, wearing spectacles and with a cravat of some sort. This man would have been standing at the back of the room and appeared to be watching over us. I showed the image to my wife, who is somewhat more a sceptic of this type of thing, but she had to admit that the image sent a shiver along her spine.

My wife and I returned to the house and took the tour again on the same day to look in the basement. We found no picture on a wall or anything that could explain the image I caught, in fact, we did not find anything that resembled anything like the image.

I will leave it with you as to what you see or believe.

Neil Kirby

Neil is a HMRC registered paramedic working for the ambulance
service in the West Midlands.
His past roles include a police officer in the West Midlands and as a
carpenter-joiner.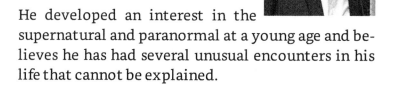

He developed an interest in the
supernatural and paranormal at a young age and be-
lieves he has had several unusual encounters in his
life that cannot be explained.

Neil is always eager to listen to new stories about
supernatural happenings around the West Midlands
and plans to write further books in order to share
them with other people.

Printed in Great Britain
by Amazon

51070905R00061